If I Had a Piece of String....

Written by
Betty Edwards, Dorothea McQueen, and Fran Martin and their students

Illustrated by R. Barnes-Murphy

MODERN CURRICULUM PRESS

Program Consultants

Becky Dugan, *Teacher*
Brady Elementary School
Little Rock, Arkansas

Debra List, *Teacher*
Hansberry Child-Parent Center
Chicago, Illinois

Judy Stobbe, *Bilingual Teacher*
Alianza School
Watsonville, California

Wanda Tansil, *Teacher*
University Terrace School
Baton Rouge, Louisiana

Executive Editor: Dorrie Berkowitz

Associate Editor: Marcia Formichelli

Design Concept: Todd Cooper/BILL SMITH STUDIO

MODERN CURRICULUM PRESS
An imprint of Paramount Supplemental Education
250 James Street
Morristown, New Jersey 07960

ISBN: 0-8136-7967-2 (single copy)   0-8136-7968-0 (6-pack)

4 5 6 7 8 9 DP 99 98 97 96 95

If I had a piece of string, I might . . .

fly a kite,

tie my shoe,

make a telephone!

If I had a piece of string, I might

make a mask,

make a necklace,

make a mobile,

go fishing!

If you had a piece of string,

what would you do?